THE LITTLE BOOK FOR COFFEE LOVERS

FELICITY HART

summersdale

THE LITTLE BOOK FOR COFFEE LOVERS

Text by Emma Marriott

An Hachette UK Company
www.hachette.co.uk

Summersdale Publishers Ltd
Part of Octopus Publishing Group Limited
Carmelite House
50 Victoria Embankment
LONDON
EC4Y 0DZ
UK

www.summersdale.com

Printed and bound in China

ISBN: 978-1-80007-984-7

Substantial discounts on bulk quantities of Summersdale books are available to corporations, professional associations and other organizations. For details contact general enquiries: telephone: +44 (0) 1243 771107 or email: enquiries@summersdale.com.

CONTENTS

INTRODUCTION

If you love a cup of coffee, then you share that passion with people across the globe. Around two billion cups of the stuff are consumed every day across every continent of the world, making coffee a truly global beverage. But how well do you know your coffee? How is it grown and what gives coffee its unique taste? You might be familiar with the names of different types of coffee drinks, but what exactly is a macchiato or a *tinto* and how do people across the world take their coffee? You might be surprised to find out!

This little book provides many of the answers and uncovers a whole host of amazing information about the mighty coffee bean. It takes a look at the extraordinary history of coffee, who first discovered its invigorating properties and how cafés and culture centred on coffee spread across the world. It provides a lowdown on the different types of coffee beans and the dizzying array of coffee drinks, from cappuccinos and cortados to flat whites and cold brew, and how you can create your favourite variation at home.

The book will also shed light on coffee around the world, from Turkish coffee and Scandinavia's "kaffeost" (coffee cheese) to the rituals and traditions that have grown around its consumption, including the Ethiopian coffee drinking ceremony *Buna Tetu*. The following pages will explain the often confusing terminology connected with coffee, as well as how you too can roast and grind your own beans, froth milk and create a latte art masterpiece at home.

The book is packed with fun facts and coffee trivia, as well as fantastic recipes with coffee as the main ingredient. They range from the super-simple coffee ice cubes and a wake-up coffee smoothie, to the eye-catching Korean Dalgona coffee and even a classic espresso martini and a tangy citrus coffee cocktail. There are also some coffee-based light bites and treats, including ice cream, creamy desserts, energy bites and crunchy biscotti that are perfect to dunk into a cup of coffee. Give them a go, explore the wonderful world of coffee and enjoy!

ALL ABOUT COFFEE

The origins of coffee are all here, from the earliest known growers in the mountains of Yemen to its eventual spread across the world. Learn also about how coffee beans are harvested, roasted and made into the wonderful array of coffees we love to drink.

BRIEF HISTORY OF COFFEE

Over the centuries, legends have emerged about who first discovered the potential of the wondrous coffee bean. One story has it that in around 850 CE, an Ethiopian goat herder, Kaldi, noticed that his goats became very energetic after eating the berries from a certain tree. When he sampled the same berries, he felt exhilarated and proclaimed his discovery to the world.

Whatever the real origin of the discovery, by the fifteenth century coffee was being grown on the mountain terraces of Yemen and was a known beverage on the Arabian Peninsula. In fact, the word coffee comes from the Arabic word *quahwah* (originally meaning wine or a drink that has stimulating effects) and by the sixteenth century the drink had reached Egypt, Persia, Syria and Turkey, where they referred to coffee as *kahveh*.

While some Islamic authorities forbade coffee because of its stimulating effects, many people liked its taste and coffee spread rapidly, with coffee houses springing up in large numbers. Here, friends and workers could meet, catch up with news, play chess and generally pass the time of day with fellow coffee lovers.

Mysterious Beverage

Travellers brought back stories of the mysterious beverage they had seen in Arab lands and in the sixteenth and seventeenth centuries coffee began to be introduced into Europe. At first the authorities were suspicious of the strange concoction, some labelling it as "the bitter invention of Satan". In 1615, the clergy condemned it in Venice until Pope Clement VIII sampled it and liked it so much he gave it his papal approval.

Coffee houses were established across Europe. Some companies, such as Lloyd's of London, evolved out of a coffee house and artists and intellectuals loved to exchange ideas over a cup of coffee. The German composer Johann Sebastian Bach was a famed coffee lover and in the 1730s even wrote a "Coffee Cantata" dedicated to his favourite drink!

By the mid-1600s coffee had arrived in the colonies of North America, but it wasn't until the Boston Tea Party of 1773, which saw Americans hurl chests of tea from ships as a protest against British taxation, that many of them switched to drinking coffee as it was deemed more patriotic.

Big Business

As its popularity spread, European powers competed to grow coffee outside Arabia. By 1700 the Dutch were growing plants in Java and other Indonesian islands, and by 1720 a French naval officer had brought coffee seedlings to the Caribbean island of Martinique. These thrived and coffee plantations rapidly spread throughout the Caribbean and South and Central America.

It's thought that coffee arrived in north-eastern Brazil in 1727 and over the following century Brazil became the world's biggest producer and exporter of coffee, as it still is today. Near perfect growing conditions resulted in extraordinary output, but it came at a human cost, as slaves manned plantations in Brazil, as they had in the Caribbean, Asia and the Americas.

By the early twentieth century, coffee was being produced on an industrial scale and big brand names were hitting the market, as was instant coffee from the 1950s onward. This in turn led to increased production of the Robusta bean in Africa and Asia. The coffee revolution, however, continues to grow with increasing interest in organic, fairtrade and sustainably grown coffee, along with an array of new flavours and coffee-making techniques.

COFFEE CHERRIES

Coffee is made from a tropical evergreen shrub or tree, the *Coffea* plant. Coffee beans are the seeds of the plant's ripened fruit, known as coffee cherries. It can take around three to four years for *Coffea* plants to bear fruit, its cherries turning bright or dark red when ripe. Within each cherry, surrounded by layers of skin and pulp, are two beans – the magic ingredient for coffee.

To turn these simple beans into coffee, the cherries are harvested, sorted and dried either in the sun or in hot-air driers, and then the seeds or coffee beans are extracted. Another method sees the beans extracted from the cherries first in a pulping machine, after which the beans are washed and dried.

The beans are then graded according to size, imperfections and their appearance, ready to be shipped. At this stage the beans are green and soft. To transform them into the dark aromatic beans familiar to coffee lovers around the world, they need to be roasted.

UNLOCKING THE FLAVOUR

Roasting brings out the aroma and flavour locked inside a bean, turning it from green to dark brown. Once roasted, the beans smell like coffee and with the moisture taken out they are lighter and crunchy to the bite, ready to be ground and brewed.

When roasting beans, coffee manufacturers first dry the green coffee beans in a rotating roasting drum at 160°C (320°F). They then raise the temperature to around 200–230°C (390–445°F) to roast the beans, before they are cooled to room temperature. The higher temperature changes the flavour and aroma of the coffee beans, and the longer the beans roast, the darker in colour they become. The perfect roast is a personal choice and can also be influenced by where you live in the world or the type of coffee you like. The main categories of roasts are:

- **Light roast** – a milder coffee taste, but with a higher caffeine content

- **Medium roast** – a stronger flavour, sometimes known as the American roast

- **Medium dark roast** – a fuller flavour with a slight bittersweet aftertaste

- **Dark roast** – a full body with a bitter taste, often given a variety of names, from Continental to Italian or French roast

ARABICA

There are over 100 different species of the *Coffea* plant, but two species, the Arabica and Robusta plants, dominate the coffee-drinking world. In fact, over 60 per cent of the coffee beans produced across the globe are the Arabica variety.

Coffee made from Arabica beans has a smoother, sweeter and more floral taste and contains less caffeine than Robusta coffee. Arabica plants are grown at high altitude, often in hilly areas where rain is plentiful. Brazil, known for its lush rainforests, is the foremost producer of Arabica coffee but it is also grown throughout Latin America, Central and East Africa, India and some parts of Indonesia.

Coffea arabica plants produce small white flowers, which have a sweet fragrance similar to jasmine flowers. While preferring a different environment to some other coffee plants, Arabica, like all species of *Coffea*, produce cherries, although their colour becomes a distinctive glossy red when ripe.

ROBUSTA

The second most popular coffee bean in the world is the Robusta bean. As the name suggests, the Robusta plant is something of a tough guy compared with the Arabica and larger too, growing up to 10 metres (32 feet). Robusta can thrive at lower altitudes and produces sweet-smelling white flowers, which develop into deep red berries. Inside these are the large and more rounded Robusta coffee beans.

The large yields that Robusta produces means that it's a cheaper coffee to produce than Arabica. Vietnam is now the world's largest exporter of Robusta, although it's also grown in Indonesia, Africa, India and Brazil.

Containing more caffeine that Arabica, Robusta coffee has a stronger smell, producing a drink that is full-bodied, with an earthy, bitter flavour, which some consider inferior to Arabica. The beans are often used in blends and instant coffee, and good-quality Robusta beans are often found in Italian espresso blends to add a fuller flavour and a better foam head (known as "crema").

LIBERICA AND EXCELSA

Unless you are a coffee connoisseur, you may never have heard of Liberica or Excelsa coffee beans. In fact, Liberica beans are difficult to get hold of in Europe and the United States, but they are popular in Asia and South America.

The trees of the Liberica can grow up to 20 metres (66 feet) and its cherries and beans are the largest of all coffee varieties. Now produced mainly in the Philippines, Indonesia and Malaysia, Liberica produces a coffee that has a strong, smoky flavour with a floral aroma and is frequently used in blends to add body and complexity. The taste of Liberica often divides coffee lovers into those who love its unusual, nutty flavour that really packs a punch and those who find its taste too harsh and bitter.

Excelsa beans are a variant of the Liberica variety. Almost exclusively grown in Southeast Asia, its oval-shaped beans produce a rich and earthy-tasting coffee, with a mild fruity taste. With such an unusual flavour, many coffee enthusiasts are eager to try it!

*Coffee smells like
freshly ground heaven.*

JESSI LANE ADAMS

Most coffee cherries contain two beans, but around five per cent of cherries contain just one, which is known as a peaberry. Some coffee lovers insist that peaberry beans produce a sweeter and more flavourful coffee, although others maintain they can't taste the difference!

TYPES OF COFFEE

There are countless ways to serve coffee, as can be seen on coffee shop menus around the world. You might be familiar with the names, but do you *really* know the difference between a macchiato and a mocha? Here's a summary of some of the most popular types, beginning with one common to all coffee drinks:

Espresso

Espresso is a concentrated form of coffee served in small, strong shots. Meaning "pressed out" in Italian, it is made by forcing nearly boiling water through finely ground coffee beans. It can be made with a wide variety of coffee beans and roasting types, although a darker roast is preferred in Italy. The resulting coffee has a dense consistency, with a strong flavour and a layer of foamy crema, which is a sign of a well-made espresso.

Espresso is made with an espresso machine and can be served on its own – each shot is typically 27 ml (1 oz). It can also be made in just 30 seconds and drunk just as quickly, making it a popular drink for those on the go!

Cappuccino

Espresso forms the base for many other coffee drinks, including the cappuccino. Typically, it contains a shot of espresso topped with steamed milk and an airy layer of milk foam.

The most important factor in making a cappuccino – and something of a test for baristas – is correctly steaming the milk so that tiny bubbles of air create a velvety texture, along with a thick milk foam on top.

The cappuccino originated in Italy where its name translates as "little hood", possibly after the brown robes of Capuchin friars, which perfectly matched the colour of espresso and frothed milk. Another theory is that the name relates to a Viennese version of the drink, the *Kapuziner*, a coffee topped with whipped cream and cinnamon, which spread in popularity across Europe in the twentieth century.

Caffe latte

A caffe latte consists of one or two shots of espresso and steamed milk, with a thin layer of foam on top. Typically, the ratio is one part espresso to three parts milk – giving the drink a creamy and light coffee taste – and the steamed milk should have a velvety texture.

Lattes are typically served in tall cups or glasses. While many coffee fans love their lattes at any time of day, Italians would normally only drink a latte or a cappuccino at breakfast or before 11 a.m. Many latte lovers like to have flavour shots added, such as vanilla, caramel or hazelnut, but some coffee purists insist on just espresso and milk.

For a refreshing alternative, an iced caffe latte is made with one or two shots of espresso, chilled milk and generous amounts of ice cubes, along with a sweetener or flavoured syrup if so desired!

Flat white and macchiato

The flat white originated in the 1980s in either Australia or New Zealand – the debate over which still rages. It is made with a double shot of espresso topped with steamed milk, usually two parts milk to one part espresso.

In a traditional flat white, the espresso should be made with half the usual amount of water and the milk should be frothed so that microbubbles form – which baristas often do by folding the milk back and forth with a spoon – to create "microfoam". The result should be a fairly strong coffee, combined with a creamy, velvety texture.

A macchiato is usually served by pouring a few teaspoons of steamed milk directly into a single shot of espresso. In Italian, macchiato translates as "stained" or "marked", as the espresso is literally marked with a tiny bit of milk. Served in a small cup or glass, it provides the caffeine kick of an espresso with just a dash of milk.

Cortado and piccolo

Coffee lovers are becoming increasingly obsessed with the cortado. They are often served in smaller cups made of metal or glass, half of which is an espresso and half steamed milk with little or no foam on top. With the cortado, the drink is less about the foam and more about the blend of flavours.

The word cortado comes from the Spanish *cortar*, "to cut", an apt name because the milk dilutes the coffee. It originated in the Basque area of Spain and then spread to northern Portugal, Cuba and across the world.

Another coffee drink served in a smaller glass or cup is the piccolo – meaning "small" in Italian. It is often made with a *ristretto* shot of espresso – which is a short shot of espresso, resulting in a more concentrated, richer flavour – topped to the brim with latte-style steamed milk.

Mocha

Another variant of the caffe latte is the caffe mocha. Like a latte, it combines espresso and steamed milk, but chocolate flavouring and sweeteners are also added in the form of chocolate syrup, cocoa powder or chocolate itself. Sometimes a mocha, also called a mochaccino, is more like a hot chocolate, with a shot of espresso added and topped with whipped cream or even a dusting of cinnamon, cocoa powder or marshmallows.

The mocha originated in the United States in the twentieth century, probably inspired by the *bicerin*, a traditional hot drink of Turin in northern Italy, which consists of layers of espresso, drinking chocolate and milk served in a small glass. Its name, however, has nothing to do with chocolate, but is from the city of Mocha in Yemen, one of the centres of the coffee trade and also a type of coffee bean.

ESPRESSO IS A MIRACLE OF CHEMISTRY IN A CUP.

Andrew Illy

Cappuccino foam should be airy, although the milk bubbles should be dense enough to stick to a spoon. The sign of a good cappuccino is that it leaves a big milk moustache after the first sip.

Americano and long black

An americano is a shot of espresso topped with hot water. Legend has it that when American soldiers were stationed in Italy during the Second World War they balked at the strong flavour of espresso, so added hot water to dilute the taste and the famous black drink was born. While this story has never been confirmed, the americano has certainly become well-known around the world, although the Italians still prefer to drink undiluted espresso, laughingly referring to the americano as "dirty water".

An americano is served without milk or cream and can also be iced with the addition of cold water and ice. A similar drink to the americano is the long black, which is popular in New Zealand and Australia. The long black is a stronger, more concentrated version of the americano, usually made by pouring a double shot of espresso over hot water, which retains the crema layer on top. The americano has a mellower flavour because hot water is added to the espresso, mixing the crema into the drink.

Cold brew

Cold brew coffee is rapidly gaining in popularity. Unlike iced coffee, cold brew is made by steeping ground coffee in cold or room-temperature water for around 12–24 hours, before straining out the grounds, then chilling it or serving as it is over ice or diluted with water.

It has a full, almost chocolatey flavour and is less acidic than other coffee drinks. On its own, cold brew can contain more caffeine than most other coffees, but it is usually diluted with water, milk or other milk substitutes.

Nitro cold brew is a variation of cold brewed coffee. Once the coffee grounds have been steeped in water, nitrogen gas is added to the mixture which gives it a creamy head of foam, similar to draft beer. The gas in the nitrogen creates pockets of air in the body of the coffee which gives it a creamy consistency – a little like a glass of Guinness – meaning that most nitro brew fans drink it black.

COFFEE AROUND THE WORLD

People around the world love to grab a coffee, whether it's first thing in the morning as a pick-me-up or later in the day with friends. The way people prepare and serve their coffee can vary hugely, both in the brewing process and in the array of unusual flavours, spices and sweeteners that can be added. Here are just a few of the different types of coffee served across the globe.

Ethiopia

Where better to start than the rumoured birthplace of the beverage, Ethiopia, the largest coffee producer in Africa and fifth largest in the world. Here, Ethiopians take the growing and drinking of coffee seriously, and have a centuries-old coffee drinking ceremony called *Buna Tetu*, meaning "come drink coffee".

The coffee is prepared in a *jebena* clay pot and participants drink three small cups, the first super-strong, the next a little milder and the last the weakest. The ceremony is about getting together with friends and family, often on a daily basis and is also observed on special occasions such as weddings.

Senegal

Coffee drinkers in the West African country of Senegal like their coffee spicy. Café Touba – named after the city of Touba – is a popular drink with a musky and intense flavour. It is made with grains of Selim, also known as djar or Guinea pepper, and cloves are sometimes added.

Roasted Robusta coffee beans are ground up with the grains of Selim and brewed using a cloth filter. Traditionally, the coffee is poured back and forth between containers to add froth and air to the liquid.

Café Touba is sometimes drunk during religious ceremonies, but it is also an everyday treat for the Senegalese – and in some other parts of West Africa – and many claim it has medicinal benefits, aiding digestion, helping with pain relief and boosting the mood.

Morocco

Morocco has a thriving café culture where Moroccans traditionally begin their day with mint tea, but many, particularly the younger generation, drink coffee as a midday or evening treat. In Moroccan cafés there are normally two types of coffee: café noir, which is a small cup of espresso; and *nous nous*, which translates as "half half" because it's half espresso and half steamed milk.

Moroccan spiced coffee is commonly prepared at home rather than in cafés. It's a type of Arabic coffee with a milder flavour, made with freshly ground coffee beans and a blend of spices, which can include nutmeg, ginger, cardamon, cinnamon and cloves. The coffee beans and spices are ground into a fine powder, which is then steeped in a coffee pot with hot water. It's often sweetened with sugar and cream.

Turkey

Turkish coffee is a sweet, delicious and intense beverage made with finely ground coffee beans, often with sugar. It should have a froth on top and is traditionally made in a small, long-handled brass or copper pot known as a *cezve*.

It is served in small cups, often with water as a palate cleanser and is sometimes flavoured with cardamom. As Turkish coffee is made with unfiltered coffee, the coffee grounds sink to the bottom of the cup. When covered with a saucer and then upturned, the shapes of the grounds are used by some for fortune telling.

Turkish coffee also plays a part in the customs surrounding Turkish weddings. Before a couple marry, the groom traditionally visits his bride's family and is served coffee prepared by his bride-to-be. As a character test, the bride sometimes uses salt instead of sugar and if the groom drinks his coffee without complaint, the bride knows her future husband will be easy-going!

Vietnam

Vietnam is one of the world's biggest exporters of coffee, second only to Brazil. Here it's all about the Robusta coffee bean, accounting for 97 per cent of all coffee produced in the country. As a result, Vietnamese coffee, *ca phe*, is made with Robusta, which some first-time drinkers liken to rocket fuel, as Robusta has around twice the caffeine content of Arabica.

In the traditional preparation of Vietnamese coffee, Robusta beans are roasted dark and mixed with other ingredients, such as chicory and corn. It is usually drunk with sweetened condensed milk, which balances out the intense flavour of the Robusta. The condensed milk is poured into the bottom of a glass then a coffee filter, known as a *phin*, is placed on top. Coffee grounds are added, hot water is poured over them, which then drips slowly into the glass.

Ca phe da, the iced version, is also popular, with the coffee dripping into a cup of ice mixed with condensed milk. Another version, known as *ca phe tru'ng*, has an egg yolk mixed into the sweetened milk to make a creamy light froth. It might seem a little odd, but devotees deem it delicious!

Coffee should be black as hell, strong as death, sweet as love.

TURKISH PROVERB

Professional tasters in the coffee industry use a "coffee flavour wheel" to help identify the incredible range of natural flavours and aromas in coffee. Basic descriptions include fruity, floral and nutty, but the wheel contains another 110 words, ranging from fennel and orange blossom, to pecan and lychee.

Brazil and South America

In Brazil, the world's biggest coffee-producing nation, it's no surprise the people love their coffee, consuming it throughout the day. Coffee is always offered to visitors and it is very much part of Brazilian culture and hospitality. *Cafezinho*, meaning "small coffee", is the most common type served in Brazil. Thick, strong and traditionally brewed with a cloth flannel filter, it is served super sweet, with sugar added during the brewing process.

Elsewhere in South America, Colombians typically like to start their morning with a *tinto* – roughly translated as "inky water" as it is a small cup of black coffee, sweetened with sugar. The traditional method of making a *tinto* is by bringing a pot of water to boil over a fire, to which you add ground coffee. In a separate pot you add unrefined sugar cane to boiling water, which you combine with the coffee.

Popular across South America is *café con leche* or "coffee with milk". Originating in Spain, a *café con leche* consists of espresso served with steamed milk. Sweet, iced *café con leche* also makes for a refreshing drink on a hot day.

Italy

Coffee-drinking is a serious business in Italy and comes with certain customs and etiquette. Italians appreciate good-quality coffee and tend only to drink a milky coffee, such as a cappuccino, for breakfast. The traditional Italian coffee pot, a moka, is a must for every Italian home and few Italians drink instant coffee.

The king of coffee in Italy is espresso, which Italians drink at any time of day. To order an espresso, you normally ask for a *caffe*, which is commonly drunk *al banco*, "at the bar", a process that takes most Italians 5 minutes max. A barista may also provide a glass of water to cleanse the palate, so you can appreciate all the flavours of the coffee. You then mix your coffee with a spoon, whether or not sugar is added and drink your espresso within 2 minutes, after which the flavours are said to dissipate. Italians tend not to hang around for too long in a café – as soon as you've necked your espresso, exchanged a few words with the barista or locals at the bar, you'll be on your way!

Scandinavia

Northern Scandinavians adore their coffee so much they've combined a meal and drink in one coffee cup! A common practice in Sweden, as well as northern Finland, Norway and parts of Russia, is to place cubes of cheese into a mug of coffee, known as *kaffeost*, "coffee cheese". The cheese hails from Swedish Lapland and was once made from reindeer milk, now usually replaced with goat's or cow's milk. The cheese has a light, sweet taste and is pre-baked and dried, so that it can absorb the coffee brew without melting.

By tradition, coffee lovers drink *kaffeost* out of birchwood mugs, spooning the cubes out of their black coffee or enjoying the little cheesy dregs left at the bottom. The rich and quite bitter flavour of the coffee is combined with creamy textures of the cheese – making for a surprisingly delicious blending of ingredients!

India

India is known for its tea cultivation and consumption, but coffee is very popular in southern India, where it is grown in the hills. The streets throng with bars serving *kaapi*, filter coffee, with a robust and fragrant flavour. *Kaapi* is made by mixing boiled milk with strong brewed coffee, usually with sugar added.

A common sight also in southern India is to see someone pouring the coffee mixture between a saucepan and mug, or from one tumbler to the other, which mixes and cools the coffee and gives it extra foam. The person pouring might hold their arm as much as a metre above the receiving vessel, giving rise to the nickname for the drink: meter coffee. While local people may be used to the practice, it makes for an extraordinary spectacle! Sometimes a customer in a coffee bar will be given a tall cup with a lip and a small empty bowl so they too can perform a mini version of the process.

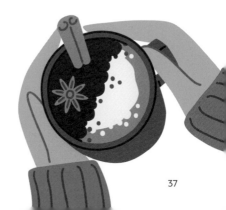

*Without my morning coffee
I'm just like a dried-up
piece of roast goat.*

JOHANN SEBASTIAN BACH

One of the most exclusive and expensive coffees in the world is *kopi luwak*. It is made from coffee cherries that have been partially digested and excreted by a small Asian mammal known as a civet or civet cat. Civets cannot digest the cherries, but they can't resist eating the ripest and most flavoursome. If you decide to give *kopi luwak* a go, make sure the coffee is sourced from a farm where the civets are treated humanely and are not battery farmed.

MAKING COFFEE

This chapter shows not only how to make the perfect cup of coffee but also how to roast your own beans and froth milk at home. It also provides a guide to the various devices and methods of making coffee and the handy bits of equipment that are a must for coffee lovers.

CAFETIERE

Also called a French press or coffee plunger, a cafetiere is usually a glass or metal container with a metal filter and plunger inside. They are super-simple to use – just add ground coffee and pour in boiling water, before using the plunger to push the grounds to the bottom of the cafetiere.

1. For a richer, fuller taste, try whole-roasted coffee beans and grind them coarsely, just before you put them in the cafetiere. You can also use pre-ground coffee beans, but ensure they are coarsely ground and preferably roasted in the last four weeks.

2. Add about 1 heaped tablespoon of ground coffee for every cup you want to make – the more you add the stronger the coffee. Boil some water – approximately 150 ml (5 fl oz) for every tablespoon of coffee – let it stand for a minute and then pour into the cafetiere.

3. Stir the mixture with a spoon and leave it to permeate for 4 minutes. Then press the plunger down slowly and firmly to the bottom. Pour the coffee and serve immediately.

MOKA POT

Moka pots are an Italian eight-sided wonder, perfect for making espresso-type coffee. They sit on a stovetop, are simple to use and can be easily transported to wherever you are going!

1. Fill the bottom chamber with cold water, place the middle chamber on top and fill with finely ground coffee. Screw the top of the moka pot onto the base.

2. Place on a stove over a medium temperature. As the water heats, pressure forces the water up through a tube to the top chamber. If the coffee is bubbling over the top, turn the heat down and make sure the stove flame is no bigger than the base of the pot.

3. After a few minutes, the coffee should have filled the upper chamber, at which point you'll hear a gurgling sound. Carefully remove the moka pot from the heat and pour the coffee.

Moka pots are similar to percolators, which also brew coffee by slowly draining, or "percolating", heated water through coffee grounds. While they function in the same way, percolators are traditionally larger, suit medium to medium-coarse ground coffee and some use an electrical heat source and switch off automatically. Please note that percolators and moka pots can get very hot when heated, even the handles can be hot to the touch, so use a cloth or potholder when you take them off the heat.

DRIPPER OR FILTER CONE

One of the simplest ways to make filter coffee, especially if you want just one cup, is the pour-over method using a dripper or filter cone. It involves pouring hot water over coffee grounds through a paper filter into a cup. The filter is placed in a dripper or filter cone (ceramic or plastic) that sits on top of the cup.

1. Boil some water, then let it rest for a couple of minutes. Place the paper filter in the dripper or cone. Put 1–2 tablespoons of medium-ground coffee in the filter, depending on the strength you like.

2. Pour a little of the hot water into the coffee to let the grounds soak it up – you'll see the grounds swell, rise and bubble, which is called "blooming".

3. Then pour in the rest of the water: start in the centre and move outward in a widening spiral. Pour it in slowly – enjoy the process and take in the heavenly aroma of coffee!

ESPRESSO MACHINE

The sound of a traditional coffee machine on the go is music to the ears of most coffee lovers, so it's not surprising many of us are investing in them for our own homes. There are a huge variety of machines on offer, all with different features and gimmicks, but the basic principle behind them is the same: pressurized water is pushed through ground coffee beans and a filter to make a shot of espresso. In using your machine, you will probably perfect your technique and water/coffee ratio, but here are some simple steps to follow when using a traditional espresso machine.

1. Fill the part of your machine that holds water and switch it on. You may have to wait anything from a few minutes to 30 minutes, but most tell you when it's ready to use. For best results, grind dark roasted coffee beans to a fine powder or use freshly ground beans.

2. Remove the portable filter from the machine and fill it with the coffee grounds. Tap and settle the grounds. Then, using a tamper (a small device with a handle), push down and compress

the coffee grounds so they have a level top. Insert and lock the filter back in and place a cup under the machine.

3. Now pull your first shot by engaging the water pressure – either by pressing a button, lever or switch – and watch as the shot flows into the cup. The ideal shot is deep brown and extraction for one espresso cup should take between 25–30 seconds, but each machine varies. A good coffee machine should produce enough pressure to create a foamy crema layer on top. Congratulations – you are now a home barista!

IF IT WASN'T FOR COFFEE, I'D HAVE NO DISCERNIBLE PERSONALITY AT ALL.

David Letterman

A person who serves coffee in a café is known as a barista. They are usually trained to make the perfect coffee and a good barista (from the Italian for "bartender") should have plenty of knowledge about the coffee-making process, from the different beans and roasts to how to change the flavour and texture of coffee.

DRIP MACHINE

A drip coffee machine also utilizes the pour-over method and makes a large jug of filtered coffee. Just switch it on and let it get to work, making satisfying gurgling noises as it does.

1. Fill up the reservoir for water, then, depending on your machine, insert a permanent mesh filter into the filter basket or a paper filter. Add freshly medium-ground beans to the filter, about a tablespoon per cup, depending on the strength you like.

2. When the coffee machine is turned on, the water, as well as the plate on which the glass jug sits, starts to heat up. As the water starts boiling, drops of water rise up through the tubing into the filter and coffee grounds and then down into the glass jug.

3. Your coffee is ready! Always rinse the mesh filter fully before using the machine again, or throw away your paper filter.

COLD BREW

No hot water? No problem, because now you can make cold brew coffee! Smooth and strong tasting, cold brew is naturally sweeter than iced coffee and is made by steeping ground coffee in cold water for 18–24 hours. You can make cold brew coffee in a variety of contraptions, but here's a good DIY version, using just a couple of jugs or large containers, a sieve and some muslin or paper towel.

1. Coarsely grind some coffee beans or use coarse-ground coffee. Place the ground coffee in the bottom of a glass jug or large container and add cold water, at roughly a 1:8 coffee to water ratio.

2. Cover the jug or put a lid on and leave the coffee to steep for 18–24 hours at room temperature.

3. Line a sieve with muslin or a few sheets of kitchen towel. Stir the coffee and then pour it through the sieve into another jug or container. Your cold brew is ready and will keep in the fridge for two to three days. You can serve it with ice, milk or sugar – it's your choice!

INSTANT

While instant coffee divides opinion among coffee lovers, it's a quick and convenient way to make coffee and is still sold in huge quantities across the globe. In fact, almost 50 per cent of the world's coffee beans are used for instant coffee.

Instant coffee is made from roasted, ground and brewed beans, and is usually a blend based on Robusta beans. The water in the beans is then removed, either by spray-drying or freeze-drying, which results in dehydrated granules. To make a coffee, you then add hot water or milk to dissolve the granules, stirring it as you do.

Another hassle-free and quick way to make a coffee is to use a coffee bag. Each bag contains ground coffee and is heat-sealed to keep it fresh. Simply add the bag to the cup, add hot water and – like a tea bag – let it infuse for 3–5 minutes, depending on how strong you like your coffee. Give the cup a stir, squeeze the bag and remove it. It's that easy and produces a coffee more reminiscent of freshly brewed coffee, and new types of coffee bags are hitting the market every day.

VACUUM COFFEE

Vacuum coffee or siphon coffee is an age-old method still popular in Japan and other parts of Asia. A typical vacuum coffee maker looks like something you might find in a science lab, consisting of an upper glass chamber, a lower glass chamber, a funnel, a filter and a heat source (usually a burner).

1. Boil around 400 ml (13 fl oz) water in a kettle and attach the filter to the bottom of the top chamber. Pour the preheated water into the bottom chamber and place it on a heat source. Balance the top chamber loosely on the bottom chamber, without sealing it, while you wait for the water to boil.

2. Coarsely grind your coffee beans, or fetch your freshly ground coffee. Once the water is boiling, attach the top chamber to the bottom chamber tightly. Water should start filling the top chamber and once it is almost full, add your coffee to it.

3. Allow the mixture to brew for 90 seconds, giving the coffee a stir halfway, then turn off the heat. The coffee should now trickle down to the bottom chamber. Remove the top chamber – remember it might be hot – and pour your coffee straightaway!

AEROPRESS

This portable device is great for making single cups of freshly brewed coffee. It consists of a cylindrical chamber and inside plunger which, when pushed down, forces water that has been sitting in ground coffee beans down through a filter. Most aeropresses have the numbers one to four on their sides, which correspond with the servings of coffee you're aiming to make.

1. Put your paper filter into the cap and twist and fit it on the chamber, nearest the number one and stand the chamber on a hardwearing mug.

2. Pour the ground coffee into the aeropress – 1-2 tablespoons of medium-ground coffee, according to your preferred taste and give it a little shake to level it out.

3. Boil some water and pour just a little onto the coffee grounds, allowing them to "bloom" for 30 seconds. Then pour in the water to a level between the numbers three and four and stir thoroughly.

4. Place the plunger on top and slowly depress it for 20–40 seconds, until you hear a hiss of air or feel resistance. That's it – your coffee is ready!

SOFT BREW

As its name suggests, soft brewing is a much gentler coffee-making process than espresso and results in a smoother, less intense tasting coffee. You'll need a soft brew pot – which is a bit like a teapot with a stainless-steel filter inside. The filter is the clever bit, as it's a very fine mesh containing thousands of tiny holes, so you can use any size of coffee grounds, even super-fine ones.

1. Place the soft brew filter inside the pot, add 1 tablespoon of ground coffee per cup.

2. Boil some water and slowly pour it into the filter container. Put the lid on and let it brew for around 4–8 minutes.

3. The coffee is ready and due to the less intense flavour, people often have less need to add milk, preferring instead to pick up on the delicate flavours of the softly brewed black coffee.

It's amazing how the world begins to change through the eyes of a cup of coffee.

DONNA A. FAVORS

Coffee is a global beverage consumed on all continents and there is even an Italian espresso machine on the International Space Station.

NITRO COLD BREW

This is a variation of cold brew coffee in which nitrogen gas is added to create a smooth texture and a foamy top. To make nitro cold brew coffee, you need a whipping siphon or whipped cream dispenser filled with nitrous oxide (N_2O).

1. First make cold brew coffee – use coarsely ground coffee (see page 51) and leave to steep at room temperature for 18–24 hours.
2. Strain the coffee through the filter and dilute with some water to your preferred concentration.
3. Pour the coffee into a whipping siphon or dispenser. Charge with one shot of nitrous oxide and give it a good shake for about 30 seconds to mix up the coffee and gas.
4. Then press the lever to release the coffee, which should be velvety and foamy and pour over ice. Nice!

TURKISH COFFEE

Turkish coffee is made with very finely ground coffee and is served in small *demitasse* cups (French for "half-cup"), similar to espresso cups, but with taller sides. It's traditionally made in a *cezve*, a small, metal Turkish coffee pot, which usually makes two small cups, and it's best to use pre-ground Turkish coffee.

1. Fill your *cezve* with cold water, add around 2 tablespoons of freshly ground coffee and, if desired, sugar.

2. Put the *cezve* on a stove top over a medium heat and after a few minutes the coffee will rise up and foam. Just before it boils, remove the *cezve* from the heat.

3. Skim off the foam, adding a little to each serving cup, then return the *cezve* to the hob and let it foam up again.

4. Pour the coffee into the serving cups, letting the foam rise to the top. Let it settle for a few minutes and serve.

COFFEE TODAY

There's an array of terminology surrounding coffee, much of it emblazoned on bags of coffee beans or café menus. Some words may be familiar, but are you crystal-clear about what they mean?

Fairtrade beans

If the coffee you buy carries the official fairtrade mark, the beans have come from a smallholder farmer who has been given a fair price for their produce. The global price of coffee is highly volatile, so the system enables farmers to earn a reliable living and offers an additional incentive to grow their coffee organically.

Single origin

This means that the coffee beans were grown and processed in the same region or location and sometimes the same farm. The term is used because the vast majority of coffees are a blend. Most producers purchase beans from different origins, then blend and roast them together. Buying single origin coffee should mean it has the characteristics unique to a specific region.

Snapchilled

Snapchilled coffee takes iced or cold-brewed coffee one step further. Brewed coffee is rapidly chilled in a special "snapchiller" machine, which immediately locks in the flavour without the coffee becoming oxidized or diluted.

Proffee

This is a favourite with gym goers and coffee lovers keen to keep up with the latest trend. Protein powder is mixed with espresso, creating a coffee that provides all the health benefits that protein gives, such as muscle repair and boosting immune response. Devotees believe proffee makes an ideal pre- and post-workout drink.

Milk alternatives

Milk alternatives have been popular for a good while now – the old favourites including almond, oat, soy and coconut milks. However, there are many new alternatives coming on to the market, all of which give unique favour. These include macadamia, pistachio and buckwheat milk, as well as potato milk in some shops.

ROASTING COFFEE BEANS AT HOME

Many coffee lovers roast their own beans to capture the flavour at its peak. Roasting the beans in a skillet or saucepan gives more control over the taste and aroma of the coffee. Here's a simple guide to roasting coffee beans at home.

1. Purchase unroasted, green coffee beans. Roasting will double their size but halve their weight.

2. Place your saucepan or skillet on a hob over a medium heat. Add the beans – no oil needed – and stir constantly.

3. After 5–10 minutes you'll see the beans turn from green to yellow, then to light and darker brown. After around 8 or 9 minutes you'll hear the first crack or pop, which usually indicates a light roasting. Roast for a further couple of minutes for a medium roast, or longer if you prefer a darker roast.

4. Transfer to a metal colander and cool, removing any chaff. Put the beans in an airlock bag, removing any air and leave for 24 hours to allow them to "de-gas" before grinding.

GRIND YOUR OWN COFFEE BEANS

To grind coffee beans, decide first on the size of grain you want. Generally, you want a coarse grain for a French press, medium-coarse for the pour-over method, medium for drip coffee, medium to fine for vacuum coffee, fine grain for espresso and very fine for Turkish coffee.

The easiest way to grind your beans – whether coarse or fine – is to use a coffee grinder. These are relatively inexpensive and simple to use. If you don't have one, try grinding your beans in a blender or food processor, although this is likely to result in a coarse or uneven grind. If all else fails, you may get better results by manually grinding your beans using one of these methods:

Pestle and mortar

Place a small quantity of beans in your mortar, mash them with the pestle, then hammer down on them until you have your preferred consistency.

Rolling pin

Put your coffee beans in a plastic freezer bag. Place on a flat surface and shake the beans out evenly. Use the rolling pin like a hammer to crack them, then roll it back and forth, applying pressure, until you get the right grind.

Don't throw away your coffee grounds as they have many practical uses at home! They contain several key minerals for plant growth so sprinkle them on soil around your plants. As they are abrasive, they can also be used as a natural cleaning scrub, ideal for scouring your sink, oven or removing food caked on pots and pans. Then, simply rinse off.

EQUIPMENT

There are a host of must-have accessories that will appeal to the coffee lover. Here's the low-down on some of them.

1. Storage – roasted beans and ground coffee quickly lose their freshness, so keep your coffee in a sealed container away from air, heat, light and moisture.

2. Kettle – try to find one with a long, thin "gooseneck" spout which allows you to pour water more precisely. Even better is to get one with variable temperature settings.

3. Cups and mugs – these depend on the type of coffee you make. Espressos are usually served in small demitasse cups. Turkish coffee is similarly served in small demitasse-size cups with tall sides. Cappuccino, mocha and americanos come in bigger, curved cups. You might want to try a cortado in a small glass tumbler.

4. Latte glasses – lattes are traditionally served in tall glasses, with handles. They should have tempered glass, as standard glass can crack or even explode when hot liquid is poured in. A double-walled coffee cup is also safer and keeps the coffee warmer for longer, but is cool to hold.

MILK FROTHING

There are a variety of ways you can froth milk at home. A steaming wand on an espresso machine creates the best foam for coffee but there are various other devices you can try – give them a whirl! First, heat the milk to no more than 71°C (160°F).

- **Handheld frother** – Move the frother up and down and side to side, until you have the desired amount of froth.

- **Hand-pump frother** – Pour your milk into the pitcher and pump up and down to create a good-quality foam.

- **Stainless-steel whisk** – whisk the milk vigorously to create a fairly thick foam.

- **Electric whisk** – whisk on a medium setting to create a more delicate froth.

- **Blender** – if your blender is plastic, make sure your milk isn't too hot (no hotter than 71°C/160°F) and blend on a medium speed.

- **Hand-held blender** – blend the milk in a deep jar as there will be a lot of spray.

- **Glass jar and lid** – pour your milk into the jar, put the lid on and shake vigorously until a thick froth forms.

- **Cafetiere** – like a hand-pump frother, pour your milk in and pump the plunger up and down.

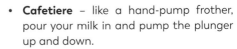

NO ONE CAN UNDERSTAND THE TRUTH UNTIL HE DRINKS OF COFFEE'S FROTHY GOODNESS.

Abdul Qadir Gilani

LATTE ART

Why not try a bit of latte art at home? You'll need an espresso machine, a steam wand to create micro-foam and a wide, shallow coffee cup. Use a pitcher or jug with a thin spout to control the flow. First make your espresso and try a heart shape – it takes practice but it's fun!

1. Steam the milk for three seconds until you see tiny bubbles on top. If there are big bubbles, tap your pitcher on the surface to remove them.

2. Tip your cup sideways and pour the milk into the middle of the espresso at a steady speed, holding the pitcher up high.

3. Once the cup is three-quarters full, lower the pitcher so the foam rises to the top. Then rock the pitcher back and forth to create a white layer on top of the brown layer, until you have a big circle of foam.

4. When the cup is full, finish your heart by pouring in a quick straight line forward.

When you've cracked the heart, why not try the leaf design featured opposite!

*I gave up coffee.
It's almost worse than
giving up a lover.*

SANDRA BULLOCK

COFFEE RECIPES

This chapter features a wide range of delicious coffee-based recipes, from smoothies, milkshakes and cocktails to sweet treats, desserts and light bites. The recipes are super simple and fun to make, all of them combining the aromatic flavour of coffee with well-known and unusual ingredients.

COFFEE MILKSHAKE

A creamy milkshake packed full of flavour and a cinch to make!

Ingredients

- 60 ml (2 fl oz) espresso
- 1 tbsp cocoa powder
- 180 ml (6 fl oz) milk
- 1 scoop vanilla ice cream

Method

Mix together the espresso, cocoa powder and milk. Then pour the coffee mixture into a blender, add the ice cream and blitz until smooth.

Pour into a glass and enjoy immediately!

For an extra treat, you could top with a generous spoonful of whipped cream and a drizzle of chocolate or caramel syrup.

CASHEW COFFEE

Blend cashews with coffee and you get a satisfying, creamy drink without adding any dairy products. For sweetness, add a dash of honey at the end.

Ingredients

- 360 ml (12.5 fl oz) strong, hot coffee
- 60 g (2 oz) cashews
  (preferably roasted and unsalted)
- Small pinch of sea salt
- Honey (optional)

Method

Blend all the ingredients for about 45 seconds, starting on a lower speed and ending on a high speed, until you have a smooth and creamy consistency.

Serve immediately or chill for later!

TURMERIC COFFEE LATTE

This perfect nourishing blend will boost your immune system. Turmeric has a wealth of health benefits and the added spices and flavours makes for a super-comforting drink.

Ingredients

- 150 ml (5 fl oz) almond milk (or milk of your choice)
- ¼ tsp ground turmeric
- ¼ tsp ground cinnamon
- ¼ tsp ground ginger
- 1 ½ tsp honey
- Black pepper
- 2 tbsp hot brewed espresso

Method

Put the milk, turmeric, cinnamon, ginger, honey and a twist of pepper in a saucepan over a gentle heat. Using a milk frother or similar, whisk until frothy.

Put the brewed espresso in a glass, top with the milk mixture and sprinkle with extra cinnamon if desired.

Turmeric has been a staple of Asian cooking for centuries and the flavours of coffee and turmeric go surprisingly well together.

WAKE-UP COFFEE SMOOTHIE

This nourishing smoothie provides everything a coffee lover needs first thing in the day. Coffee, whole grains and banana – and you can even add almond, peanut or other nut butter for some protein or healthy fats.

Ingredients

- 120 ml (4 fl oz) chilled coffee or cold brew coffee
- 1 banana, sliced and frozen
- 25 g (0.5 oz) rolled oats
- 120 ml (4 fl oz) milk
- 1 tbsp nut butter (optional)

Method

Put all the ingredients in a blender and whiz up until smooth and creamy.

Serve straightaway, enjoy and power on with your day!

ICED COFFEE LEMONADE

Lemonade and coffee might seem like an odd combination, but they go surprisingly well together and produce a tangy, refreshing drink. Here's how to make a glass of the good stuff.

Ingredients

- Ice
- 240 ml (8 fl oz) very strong coffee
- 120 ml (4 fl oz) lemonade – either homemade (by combining sugar, water and lemon juice) or ready-made
- Splash of sparkling water
- Slice of lemon (optional)

Method

Fill a glass with ice and pour in the coffee.

Add the lemonade – approximately 1 part lemonade to 1 part coffee – or to taste.

Add a splash of sparkling water and a slice of lemon, and have a nice day!

COFFEE ICE CUBES
Makes 16

Take your iced coffee one step further and make coffee ice cubes. Simply add to milk, hot water or to your iced coffee for extra flavour!

Ingredients

- 400 ml (13 fl oz) brewed coffee
- Ice-cube tray

Method

Brew your coffee and then allow to cool for 30–60 minutes.

Carefully pour the coffee into the ice cube tray. Place in the freezer for 3–4 hours and that's it!

> If you can, use a silicone ice cube tray, rather than a plastic one, as it's easier to remove the ice cubes when frozen.

DALGONA COFFEE

This eye-catching coffee from South Korea has become a global trend. Frothy coffee sits on top of a layer of milk, like an upside-down cappuccino and it's really simple to make.

Ingredients

- 1–2 tbsp instant coffee
- ½ tbsp sugar
- 250 ml (8 fl oz) milk

Method

In a mixing bowl, combine the instant coffee and sugar with 2 tbsp of hot water.

Then, using an electric hand whisk, whisk the mixture until it froths, becomes a pale toffee colour and stiff peaks form when the whisk is removed.

Heat the milk if preferred and pour into a heatproof glass. Spoon dollops of the coffee on top, smooth out and take a photo of your creation!

GINGERBREAD LATTE

This makes for a perfect drink at Christmas, brimming with all the flavours of the holiday season. Grab those spices and give it a go!

Ingredients

- 300 ml (10 fl oz) whole milk
- ½ tsp ground ginger
- Pinch of nutmeg, plus a little extra
- Pinch of ground cinnamon
- ¼ tsp vanilla extract
- 1 tbsp soft brown sugar
- 1 shot hot espresso
- Whipped cream (optional)

Method

Put the milk, spices, vanilla extract and sugar in a small saucepan. Place on a medium-high heat, stirring all the time, until steaming.

Put the espresso in a tall glass or mug and pour in the spiced milk. Top with whipped cream and perhaps an extra sprinkle of nutmeg.

Why not add a mini gingerbread man on top!

COFFEE LASSI

Lassi is a traditional yogurt drink popular in North India. It's often flavoured with spices and fruit and can be savoury or sweet. Here we add coffee, maple syrup and a pinch of cardamom.

Ingredients

- 30 ml (1 fl oz) chilled espresso
- 50 ml (2 fl oz) yogurt
- 150 ml (5 fl oz) milk
- Tiny pinch of cardamom
- 1 tsp maple syrup
- Chocolate powder or flakes (optional)

Method

Place all the ingredients in a blender and give it a whizz, until you have a smooth and creamy consistency.

Pour into a small glass, sprinkle on some chocolate flakes or powder and savour the creamy flavours of a lassi.

COLA ICED COFFEE

The sweetness of cola contrasts brilliantly with the more bitter coffee. In Brazil, they would add chocolate milk for a creamier texture.

Ingredients

- Ice cubes
- 150 ml (5 fl oz) cola
- 1 shot espresso
- Syrup to taste

Method

Fill a glass with ice cubes. Pour in the cola and then the espresso. Add syrup if you want some extra sweetness and stir – that's all there is to it!

COFFEE BEAN VODKA

A delicious, home-made type of coffee liqueur, with a strong coffee bean flavour, without being oversweet. You can add it to strong black coffee, cocktails or sweet treats, but remember this is for adults only.

Ingredients

- 30 coffee beans
- 1 tsp sugar
- 450 ml (15 fl oz) vodka

Method

Tip the coffee beans into a bowl and, with the back of a metal spoon, crush them until they are cracked and broken.

Pour the coffee beans into a sterilized preserving jar with a metal lid, sprinkle on the sugar and add the vodka.

Seal and gently shake. Store in a cool, dark place, swirling the contents of the jar daily for four days. Then strain and bottle. For a late-night treat, add to hot black coffee with whipped cream and sprinkle on some cinnamon.

ESPRESSO MARTINI

This classic coffee cocktail is best served in a chilled martini glass. It's made using a cocktail shaker and strainer – so is also fun to create!

Ingredients

- 80 ml (3 fl oz) coffee bean vodka (see previous page)
- 30 ml (1 fl oz) espresso, chilled
- 5 ice cubes
- 3 coffee beans (optional)

Method

Put your martini glass in the fridge to chill.

Pour the coffee bean vodka and espresso into the cocktail shaker. Add the ice cubes and – here comes the fun bit – shake vigorously for 8–10 seconds.

Strain the drink into the martini glass, top with the coffee beans and take that first sip.

The espresso martini is a relatively recent invention by a London bartender in 1983 who was asked by a customer to make a drink that would wake her up.

CITRUS COFFEE COCKTAIL

You'll need a cocktail shaker and highball glass for this bright and breezy cocktail, with a delicious coffee and citrus tang.

Ingredients

- 100 ml (3.5 fl oz) brewed coffee, cooled
- 1 tsp Irish cream liqueur
- 1 tsp orange liqueur
- Pinch of cinnamon
- Ice cubes
- Orange peel, to garnish

Method

Put the coffee, the liqueurs and cinnamon in the cocktail shaker and shake for a good 8–10 seconds.

Fill a highball glass with ice, pour in the cocktail and beautify with curls of orange peel.

This cocktail is an all-year-round winner, perfect for summer and Christmas parties.

IRISH COFFEE

This is the ultimate warming drink that was traditionally served at the end of a meal and has travelled from its homeland in Ireland across the world.

Ingredients

- 2 tbsp double cream
- 150 ml (5 fl oz) freshly brewed black coffee
- 50 ml (2 fl oz) Irish whiskey
- 1 tsp brown sugar (or to taste)
- Freshly grated nutmeg

Method

Lightly whip the double cream and set to one side.

Pour the hot coffee into a heatproof glass, add the whiskey and sugar and stir until the sugar has dissolved.

Gently float the cream on top, dust over some nutmeg and sit back, relax and enjoy!

VIETNAMESE EGG COFFEE

This dessert coffee is made with condensed milk and egg. Don't knock it until you've tried it, as the strong coffee works brilliantly with the luxuriant and creamy topping.

Ingredients

- 1 tbsp condensed milk
- 1 egg yolk*
- 60 ml (2 fl oz) espresso
- Cocoa or chocolate powder (optional)

Method

In a bowl, whisk together the condensed milk and egg yolk until it forms a thick, cake-batter-like foam.

Pour the espresso into a small cup or glass, gently spoon the egg foam on top and dust with the cocoa or chocolate powder, if desired.

Some people describe this delicious beverage as a tiramisu in drink form!

* Consuming raw egg poses an increased risk of salmonella.

COFFEE ICE CREAM
Makes eight servings

A dreamy and super-easy recipe for coffee and ice-cream lovers alike! Instead of pecans, you could sprinkle on crushed walnuts, chocolate chips or even a dash of coffee liqueur.

Ingredients

- 2 tbsp instant coffee granules
- 350 ml (12 fl oz) double cream
- 200 ml (7 fl oz) condensed milk
- Chopped pecans (optional)

Method

Mix the coffee with 2 tbsp of water. Then pour into a bowl and whisk with the cream and condensed milk until thick and creamy.

Place in an airtight container, sprinkle on your preferred topping and freeze for 6 hours or overnight.

Serve with whipped cream, chocolate sauce or even some crunchy amaretto cookies. Yum.

COFFEE AND CHOCOLATE ENERGY BITES
Makes 12

These are great sweet treats when you're on the go or as a healthier dessert option. You could substitute the cashews with almonds, walnuts or pecans.

Ingredients

- 140 g (5 oz) raw cashews
- 3 tbsp coffee beans or ground coffee
- 225 g (8 oz) soft, pitted dates
- 35 g (1 oz) dark chocolate or chocolate chips

Method

Put the cashews and coffee beans in a food processor and mix until it is a coarse, grainy consistency. Add the dates and process until you have a thick, sticky dough – if the mixture is a little crumbly, add 1 tsp of warm water.

Add the chocolate and process briefly to mix in. Remove the dough and, using your hands, roll into 12 balls and you're ready to go – no baking required!

MOCHA FUDGE
Makes 20

This creamy, chocolatey fudge is combined with coffee and has a nutty crunch – what's not to love!

Ingredients

- 150 g (5 oz) dark chocolate
- 200 g (7 oz) white chocolate
- 300 ml (10 fl oz) condensed milk
- 50 g (2 oz) butter
- 2 tbsp instant coffee granules,
  dissolved in 1 tbsp water
- 50 g (2 oz) chopped almonds,
  plus a little extra to sprinkle on top (optional)

Method

Break up the chocolate into small pieces and place into a heatproof bowl with the condensed milk and butter.

Place the bowl on top of a pan of hot water on the stove and heat until the chocolate has melted.

Add the coffee and stir in the chopped almonds if using.

Pour into a buttered dish and cool overnight to set, before cutting into pieces. If desired, sprinkle some chopped almonds on top. Heaven!

AFFOGATO

This creamy Italian dessert is made by combining hot coffee with ice cream. It's delicious on its own or you could add a tasty topping, such as caramel sauce, chocolate shavings, chopped hazelnuts or even crushed amaretti biscuits.

Ingredients

- 50 ml (2 fl oz) hot espresso coffee
- 1 scoop good-quality vanilla ice cream
- Topping of your choice (optional)

Method

Put a scoop of the ice cream into a small glass or bowl and pour a shot of the hot espresso over it. Serve it straightaway, stirring the ice cream so it melts a little.

Pour over or sprinkle on the topping of your choice (if using).

> Affogato means "drowned" in Italian as the ice cream is drowned in coffee!

ALMOND AND COFFEE BISCOTTI
Makes 20

These crunchy biscotti are perfect for dunking in a cup of coffee and they contain less sugar than normal cookies. Hazelnuts, pecans or other nuts also work well.

Ingredients

- 300 g (10 oz) plain flour
- 2 tsp baking powder
- 90 g (3 oz) caster sugar
- 75 g (2.5 oz) ground almonds
- 30 g (1 oz) flaked almonds
- 4 tsp instant coffee, dissolved in 4 tsp boiling water, cooled
- 2 eggs
- 2 egg whites

Method

Preheat the oven to 180°C (350°F). Line two baking trays with baking paper.

In a medium bowl, combine the flour, baking powder, sugar and almonds. Pour in the coffee, eggs and egg whites and stir until the mixture forms a dough.

Place the dough on a lightly floured work surface and shape into two 2-cm (3/4 in.) thick logs, each about 10 x 15 cm (4 x 6 in.).

Place on the baking trays and bake for 25 minutes. Remove from the oven, turn the temperature down to

150°C (300°F). Once the logs have cooled slightly, cut into slices about 1 cm thick.

Place slices back on the baking trays and return to the oven for approximately 30 minutes, turning after 15 minutes, until beautifully crisp and crunchy.

In Italian, biscotti, like the word "biscuit", means baked twice.

COFFEE AND WALNUT FLAPJACKS
Makes 20

These sweet and sticky flapjacks will satisfy those coffee cravings. Enjoy them on their own or topped with coffee and walnut icing (see page 114).

Ingredients

- 280 g (10 oz) butter
- 100 ml (3 fl oz) espresso or strong coffee
- 85 g (3 oz) dark brown soft sugar
- 100 g (3.5 oz) golden syrup
- 100 g (3.5 oz) walnut pieces
- 175 g (6 oz) rolled porridge oats
- 175 g (6 oz) whole porridge oats
- 100 g (3.5 oz) plain flour
- Pinch of salt

Method

Line a 20 x 30 cm (8 x 12 in.) cake tin with baking parchment and heat oven to 190°C/370°F.

In a small saucepan, melt the butter and add the coffee, sugar and syrup. Stir in the remaining ingredients until the sugar has dissolved.

Press into the cake tin, bake for 25 minutes and then leave to cool. Then either top with icing (see page 114) or turn out onto a chopping board and cut into squares.

COFFEE AND WALNUT ICING

This icing can be used to top the flapjacks on page 112, or any cupcake or bake, adding a further coffee kick and creamy sweetness.

Ingredients

- 75 g (3 oz) butter
- 3 tbsp espresso or hot strong coffee
- 350 g (12 oz) icing sugar
- 20 walnut halves,
  plus 2 tbsp finely chopped walnuts

Method

In a small saucepan, melt the butter and coffee, then stir in the icing sugar.

If icing the flapjacks, wait until they have cooled and then spread on the icing. Top with the walnut halves and scatter over the finely chopped walnuts. Leave for the icing to set and firm up before serving.

JAPANESE COFFEE JELLY
Makes two servings

Why should kids have all the fun?! Coffee jelly is a popular treat in Japan, where it is enjoyed alongside, or instead of, a cup of coffee, or as a dessert served with sweetened milk or whipped cream.

Ingredients

- 1 tbsp unflavoured gelatine powder
- 60 ml (2 fl oz) water
- 470 ml (16 fl oz) strong brewed coffee or espresso
- 2 tbsp sugar

Method

In a small bowl, combine the gelatine powder and water.

Put the coffee and sugar in a saucepan over a medium-to-high heat and bring to a near boil.

Turn the heat off and whisk in the gelatine mixture until it dissolves. Set aside to cool for about 15 minutes.

Pour into a dish and refrigerate for about 5 hours or overnight. Once set, cut the jelly into cubes and serve either as a snack or dessert. Go make your friends jelly-ous...

TIRAMISU
Makes eight servings

A classic boozy dessert which is soothingly creamy, but packs a coffee punch. Originally from Italy and popular all over the world.

Ingredients

- 75 ml (2.5 fl oz) Marsala
- 75 g (2.5 oz) caster sugar
- 500 ml (1 pint) whipping cream
- 250 g (8 oz) mascarpone
- 250 ml (8 fl oz) strong coffee
- 150 g (5 oz) sponge fingers
- 2 tbsp cocoa powder

Method

Put the Marsala, sugar, cream and mascarpone in a large mixing bowl and whisk until it is thick and smooth.

Pour the coffee into a large shallow container and add the sponge fingers, turning them to soak up the coffee. After a few seconds, remove the fingers and layer in a large glass serving bowl.

Spread the mascarpone mixture on top and sift over the cocoa powder. Chill for 30 minutes and serve. A perfect post-dinner pick-me-up (the translation of tira-mi-su in Italian!).

COFFEE GRANITA
Makes four servings

Coffee granita is a refreshing, crunchy dessert particularly popular in Sicily, Italy. The coffee-flavoured crystals provide the perfect summer pick-me-up.

Ingredients

- 110 g (4 oz) granulated sugar
- 570 ml (1 pint) strong espresso coffee or filter coffee
- Whipped cream (optional)

Method

Mix the sugar into the hot coffee and let it dissolve. Allow it to cool and then pour into a plastic freezer container.

Place in the freezer and after around 2–3 hours, or when crystals have begun to form, stir it with a fork. Return to the freezer and keep forking the crystals, until there is no liquid coffee left.

Twenty minutes before serving, place it in the fridge then break it up with a fork. Serve in a glass or small bowl, topped with whipped cream if preferred and relive that Italian holiday!

Some research suggests your skin might benefit from drinking coffee! The caffeine in coffee might improve blood circulation in the skin and leftover coffee grounds can work as a DIY skin scrub, exfoliating your skin and lifting off dead skin cells to make your skin feel smoother and brighter. Combine equal parts coffee grounds with brown sugar and a squeeze of fresh lemon juice, and gently rub on your skin. Let it sit on the skin for a few minutes, then rinse off.

LAST WORD

So now you know all about the good people who first came across the wonders of the coffee bean and how it spread across the world. You've delved into the whole coffee-making process, from coffee plant to the aromatic brew we all love and, finally, you can make sense of that long list of coffees on offer at your local café.

You can arm yourself with the perfect coffee-making device and recreate your favourite drink at home like a fully fledged barista. You can even roast your beans, foam up your milk – the fun to be had is endless! And if you're still craving that coffee taste, you can whip up a whole load of coffee-based drinks and desserts.

So go forth and give that new recipe a go – try a cashew coffee, a soft brew or a lassi and enjoy the frothy goodness of coffee!

TODAY'S GOOD MOOD IS SPONSORED BY COFFEE.

RECIPE INDEX

IMAGE CREDITS

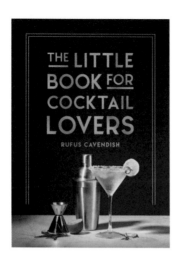

The Little Book for Cocktail Lovers
Rufus Cavendish

Hardback

978-1-80007-983-0

Discover everything you need to know to become the ultimate cocktail connoisseur with this pocket guide. Packed within these pages is a selection of showstopper recipes to suit every taste bud, plus craft ideas to add sparkle to your soirées. With a dash of trivia and a healthy measure of fun, it's time to make every hour cocktail hour!

Have you enjoyed this book?

If so, find us on Facebook at
Summersdale Publishers, on Twitter at
@Summersdale and on Instagram and TikTok at
@summersdalebooks and get in touch.

We'd love to hear from you!

www.summersdale.com